The Old North State Fact Book

Division of Archives and History
North Carolina Department of Cultural Resources
Fourth Revised Edition
Second Printing, 1995

Copyright, 1990, by the North Carolina Division of Archives and History

ISBN 0-86526-248-9

CONTENTS

FOREWORD

The *North Carolina Manual*, issued biennially by the Office of the Secretary of State, includes an introductory chapter giving information on the state's history, the State Capitol, state flag, seal, flower, bird, and other similar topics. Because the Historical Publications Section of the Division of Archives and History, North Carolina Department of Cultural Resources, frequently receives requests for such information from curious schoolchildren and interested citizens, an arrangement was made a number of years ago to publish portions of the first part of the *Manual* as a separate booklet under the title *The Old North State Fact Book*.

The Division of Archives and History wishes to thank Secretary of State Rufus L. Edmisten and his director of publications, Julie Snee, for their cooperation in making possible several editions of this pamphlet. This new edition is printed from the 1991-1992 *North Carolina Manual*.

Joe A. Mobley, *Acting Administrator*
Historical Publications Section

October 1995

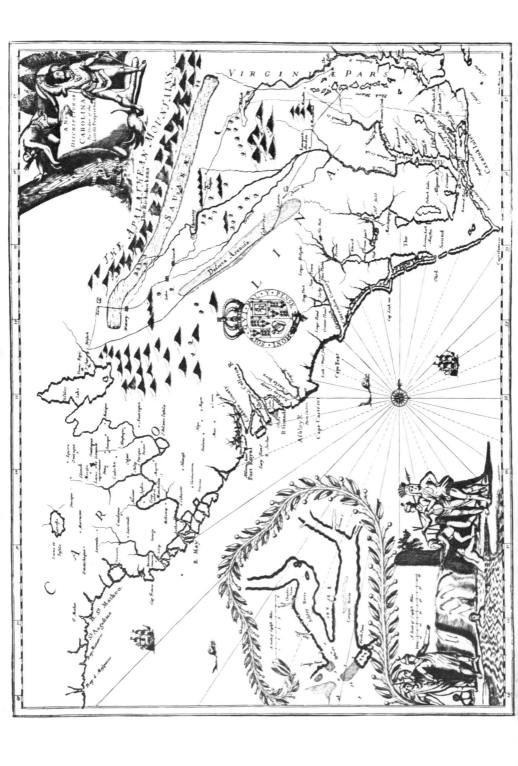

AN EARLY HISTORY OF NORTH CAROLINA

The first known European exploration of North Carolina occurred during the summer of 1524. A Florentine navigator named Giovanni da Verrazano, in the service of France, explored the coastal area of North Carolina between the Cape Fear River area and Kitty Hawk. A report of his findings was sent to Francis I, and published in Richard Hakluyt's *Divers Voyages touching the Discoverie of America*. No attempt was made to colonize the area.

Between 1540 and 1570 several Spanish explorers from the Florida Gulf region explored portions of North Carolina, but again no permanent settlements were established.

Coastal North Carolina was the scene of the first attempt to colonize America by English-speaking people. Two colonies were begun in the 1580's under a charter granted by Queen Elizabeth to Sir Walter Raleigh. The first colony, established in 1585 under the leadership of Ralph Lane, ended in failure.

A second expedition under the leadership of John White began in the spring of 1587 when 110 settlers, including seventeen women and nine children, set sail for the new world. The White Colony arrived near Hatteras in June, 1587, and went on to Roanoke Island, where they found the houses built by Ralph Lane's expedition still standing. Two significant events occurred shortly after the colonist's arrival—two "friendly" Indians were baptized and a child was born. Virginia Dare, as the baby was named, became the first child born to English-speaking parents in the new world. The colonists faced many problems. As supplies ran short White was pressured to return to England for provisions. Once in England, White was unable to immediately return to Roanoke because of an impending attack by the Spanish Armada. When he was finally able to return in 1590, he found only the remnants of what was once a settlement. There were no signs of life, only the word "CROATAN" carved on a nearby tree. Much

speculation has been made about the fate of the "Lost Colony," but no one has successfully explained the disappearance of the colony and its settlers.

The first permanent English settlers in North Carolina were immigrants from the tidewater area of southeastern Virginia. These first of these "overflow" settlers moved into the Albemarle area of northeast North Carolina around 1650.

In 1663, Charles II granted a charter to eight English gentlemen who had helped him regain the throne of England. The charter document contains the following description of the territory which the eight Lords Proprietors were granted title to:

> All that Territory or tract of ground, situate, lying, and being within our Dominions in America, extending from the North end of the Island called Luck Island, which lies in the Southern Virginia Seas and within six and Thirty degrees of the Northern Latitude, and to the West as far as the South Seas; and so Southerly as far as the River Saint Mathias, which borders upon the Coast of Florida, and within one and Thirty degrees of Northern Latitude, and West in a direct Line as far as the South Seas aforesaid; Together with all and singular Ports, Harbours, Bays, Rivers, Isles, and Islets belonging unto the Country aforesaid; And also, all the Soil, Lands, Fields, Woods, Mountains, Farms, Lakes, Rivers, Bays, and Islets situate or being within the Bounds or Limits aforesaid; with the Fishing of all sorts of Fish, Whales, Sturgeons, and all other Royal Fishes in the Sea, Bays, Islets, and Rivers within the premises, and the Fish therein taken;
>
> And moreover, all Veins, Mines, and Quarries, as well discovered as not discovered, of Gold, Silver, Gems, and precious Stones, and all other, whatsoever be it, of Stones, Metals, or any other thing whatsoever found or to be found within the Country, Isles, and Limits . . . ."

The territory was to be called Carolina in honor of Charles the First. In 1665, a second charter was granted in order to clarify territorial questions not answered in the first charter. This charter extended the boundry lines of Carolina to include:

> All that Province, Territory, or Tract of ground, situate, lying, and being within our Dominions of America aforesaid, extending North and Eastward as far as the North end of Carahtuke River or Gullet; upon a straight Westerly line to Wyonoake Creek, which lies within or about the degrees of thirty six and thirty Minutes, Northern latitude, and so West in a direct line as far as the South Seas; and South and Westward as far as the degrees of twenty nine, inclusive, northern latitude; and so West in a direct line as far as the South Seas.

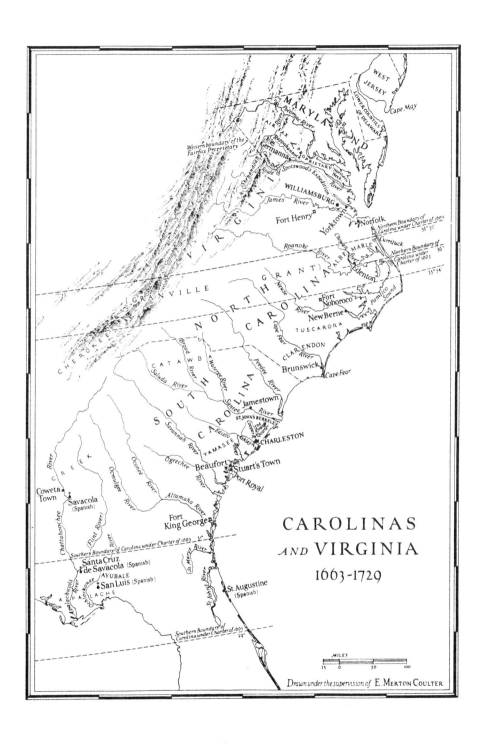

WEST
JERSEY
Cape May
LOWER COUNTIES OF DELAWARE

MARYLAND

Potomac River
Western boundary of the Fairfax Proprietary
Germanna
FAIRFAX
Rappahannock River
PROPRIETARY
Northern Neck
Route of Spotswood's Expedition

V I R G I N I A

WILLIAMSBURG
James River
Fort Henry

Yorktown
Norfolk
Northern Boundary of Carolina under Charter of 1665
36° 30'

Roanoke
River
ALBEMARLE
Currituck
Northern Boundary of Carolina under Charter of 1663
36°
Chowan River
Edenton

N O R T H   C A R O L I N A
(G R A N T)
35° 34'

G R A N V I L L E
Neuse
River
Fort
Nohoroco
New Berne
Pamlico Sound

C H E R O K E E

TUSCARORA

Cape Fear River
CLARENDON
Brunswick
Cape Fear

S O U T H   C A R O L I N A
CATAWBA
Broad River
Saluda River
Wateree River
Santee River
Peedee River

Savannah River
Edisto River
Congaree River
Cooper River
ST. JOHN'S BERKELEY
Jamestown
CHARLESTON
YAMASEE
Ashley River

C R E E K
River
Ocmulgee River
Oconee River
Ogeechee River
Beaufort
Stuart's Town
Port Royal

Coweta
Town
Savacola
(Spanish)

Altamaha River
Fort
King George

Chattahoochee River
Flint River

Southern Boundary of Carolina under Charter of 1665
31°
St. Marys River

Santa Cruz
de Savacola (Spanish)
AYUBALE
San Luis (Spanish)
APALACHE
Apalachicola River
Ochlockonee River

St. Johns River
St. Augustine
(Spanish)

CAROLINAS
AND VIRGINIA
1663-1729

Southern Boundary of
Carolina under Charter of 1665
29°

MILES
15   0   50   100

Drawn under the supervision of E. MERTON COULTER

Between 1663 and 1729, North Carolina was under the control of the Lords Proprietors and their descendents who commissioned colonial officials and authorized the governor and his council to grant lands in the name of the Lords Proprietors. In 1669, John Locke wrote the Fundamental Constitutions as a model for the government of Carolina. Albemarle County was divided into local governmental units called precincts. Initially there were three precincts—Berkley, Carteret, and Shaftesbury—but as the colony expanded to the south and west new precincts were created. By 1729, there were a total of eleven precincts—six in Albemarle County and five in Bath County which had been created in 1696. Although the Albemarle Region was the first permanent settlement in the Carolina Area, another region was developed around present-day Charleston, South Carolina. Because of the natural harbor and easier access to trade with the West Indies, more attention was given to developing the Charleston area than her northern counterparts. For a twenty-year period, 1692-1712, the colonies of North and South Carolina existed as one unit of government. Although North Carolina still had her own assembly and council, the governor of Carolina resided in Charleston and a deputy governor was appointed for North Carolina.

In 1729, seven of the Lords Proprietors sold their interest in North Carolina to the Crown and North Carolina became a royal colony. The eighth proprietor, Lord Granville, retained economic interest and continued granting land in the northern half of North Carolina. All political functions were under the supervision of the crown until 1775.

Colonial government in North Carolina was essentially the same during both the proprietory and royal periods, the only major difference being who appointed colonial officials. There were two primary units of government: the governor and his council, and the colonial assembly made up of persons elected by the qualified voters of the county. There were also colonial courts; however, unlike today's courts, they were rarely involved in formulating policy. All colonial officials were appointed by either the Lords Proprietors prior to 1729, or by the crown afterwards. Members of the colonial assembly were elected from the various precincts (counties) and from certain towns which had been granted representation. The term "precinct" as a geographical unit ceased to exist after 1735. These areas became known as "counties" and about the same time "Albemarle County" and "Bath County" ceased to exist as governmental units.

The governor was an appointed official, as were the colonial secretary, attorney general, surveyor general, and the receiver general. All officials served at the pleasure of the Lords Proprietors or the crown. During the proprietory period, the council was comprised of appointed persons who were to look after the proprietors' interests in the new world. The council served as an advisory group to the governor during the proprietary and royal periods, as well as serving as the upper house of the legislature when the assembly was in session. When vacancies occurred in colonial offices or on the council, the governor was authorized to carry out all mandates of the proprietors, and could make a temporary appointment until the vacancy was filled by proprietory or royal commission. One member of the council was chosen as president of the group, and many council members were also colonial officials. If a governor or deputy governor was unable to carry on as chief executive because of illness, death, resignation, or absence from the colony, the president of the council became the chief executive and exercised all powers of the governor until the governor returned or a new governor was commissioned.

The colonial assembly was made up of men elected from each precinct and town where representation had been granted. Not all counties were entitled to the same number of representatives. Many of the older counties had five representatives each while those newer ones formed after 1696 were each allowed only two. Each town granted representation was allowed one representative. The presiding officer of the colonial assembly was called the speaker and was elected from the entire membership of the house. When a vacancy occurred, a new election was ordered by the speaker to fill it. On the final day of each session, the bills passed by the legislature were signed by both the speaker and the president of the council.

The colonial assembly could not meet arbitrarily, but rather convened only when called into session by the governor. Being the only body authorized to grant a salary to the governor or to be responsible for spending tax monies, the legislature met on a regular basis until just before the Revolutionary War. However, there was a constant battle for authority between the governor and his council on the one hand and the general assembly on the other. Two of the most explosive issues were the power of the purse and the electing of the treasurer, both privileges of the assembly. Another issue which raised itself was who had the authority to create new counties. On more than one occasion, elected representatives from counties created by the governor and council, without consultation and proper legislative action by the lower house, were refused seats until the matter was resolved. These conflicts between the executive and legislative bodies were to have a profound effect on the organization of state government after Independence.

North Carolina, on April 12, 1776, authorized her delegates to the Continental Congress to vote for independence. This was the first official action by a Colony calling for independence. The 83 delegates present in Halifax at the Fourth Provincial Congress unanimously adopted the Halifax Resolves, which read as follows:

> The Select Committee taking into Consideration the usurpations and violences attempted and committed by the King and Parliament of Britain against America, and the further Measures to be taken for frustrating the same, and for the better defence of this province reported as follows, to wit,
>
> "It appears to your Committee that pursuant to the Plan concerted by the British Ministry for subjugating America, the King and Parliament of Great Britain have usurped a Power over the Persons and Properties of the People unlimited and uncontrouled and disregarding their humble Petitions for Peace, Liberty and safety, have made divers Legislative Acts, denouncing War

Joseph Hewes

North Carolina Signers of the Declaration of Independence

William Hooper

John Penn

Famine and every Species of Calamity daily employed in destroy-
ing the People and committing the most horrid devastations on
the Country. That Governors in different Colonies have declared
Protection to Slaves who should imbrue their Hands in the Blood
of their Masters. That the Ships belonging to America are declared
prizes of War and many of them have been violently seized and
confiscated in consequence of which multitudes of the people
have been destrlyed or from easy Circumstances reduced to the
most Lamentable distress.

And whereas the moderation hitherto manifested by the United
Colonies and their sincere desire to be reconciled to the mother
Country on Constitutional Principles, have procured no mitigation
of the aforesaid Wrongs and usurpations and no hopes remain of
obtaining redress by those Means alone which have been hitherto
tried, Your Committee are of Opinion that the house should enter
into the following Resolve, to wit

Resolved that the delegates for this Colony in the Continental
Congress be impowered to concur with the other delegates of the
other Colonies in declaring Independency, and forming foreign
Alliances, resolving to this Colony the Sole, and Exclusive right
of forming a Constitution and Laws for this Colony, and of
appointing delegates from time to time (under the direction of a
general Representation thereof) to meet the delegates of the other
Colonies for such purposes as shall be hereafter pointed out.

The Halifax Resolves were not only important because they were the first
official action calling for independence, but also because they were not a
unilateral recommendation. They were instead recommendations directed to
all the colonies and their delegates assembled at the Continental Congress
in Philadelphia. Virginia followed with her own recommendations soon after
the adoption of the Halifax Resolution and eventually on July 4, the final
draft of the Declaration of Independence was signed. William Hooper,
Joseph Hewes, and John Penn were the delegates from North Carolina who
signed the Declaration of Independence.

In early December, 1776, delegates to the Fifth Provincial Congress adopted
the first constitution for North Carolina. On December 21, 1776, Richard
Caswell became the first governor of North Carolina under the new constitution. On November 21, 1789, the state adopted the United States Constitution, becoming the twelfth state to enter the Federal Union. In 1788, North
Carolina had rejected the Constitution because of the lack of necessary
amendments to ensure freedom of the people.

A Constitutional convention was held in 1835 and among several changes
made in the Constitution was the method of electing the governor. After this
change, the governor was elected by the people for a term of two years
instead of being elected by the legislature for one year. Edward Bishop
Dudley was the first governor elected by the people.

In 1868, a second constitution which drastically altered North Carolina
Government was adopted. For the first time, all major state officers were

8

Led by Mrs. Penelope Barker, wife of Thomas Barker who served as agent for North Carolina in London, 51 ladies of Edenton gathered on October 25, 1774, to show their support for the colony's opposition to the tea tax. These couragous women wore no disguises as had the participants in the Boston Tea Party some ten months earlier, but rather openly declared their patriotism by signing an agreement to support whatever the men of the colony were doing for the peace and happiness of their country. This action was one of the earliest known political efforts by women in America. The above caricature was published in the London newspapers along with an account of the event.

elected by the people. The governor and other executive officers were elected to four-year terms; while the justices of the supreme court and judges of the superior court were elected to eight-year terms. The members of the General Assembly continued to be elected for two-year terms. Between 1868 and 1970 numerous amendments were incorporated into the 1868 constitution, so that in 1970, the people voted to adopt a completely new constitution. Since then, several amendments have been ratified but one in particular is a break from the past. In 1977, the people voted to allow the governor and lieutenant governor to run for reelection successively for an additional term.

North Carolina has had two permanent capitals, New Bern and Raleigh, and there have been three capitol buildings. Tryon Palace in New Bern was constructed in the period 1767-1770, and the main building was destroyed by fire February 27, 1798. The first capitol in Raleigh was completed in 1794 and was destroyed by fire on June 21, 1831. The present capitol building was completed in 1840.

In 1790, North Carolina ceded her western lands which included Washington, Davidson, Hawkins, Greene, Sullivan, Sumner, and Tennessee counties, to the Federal government. Between 1790 and 1796 the territory was known as Tennessee Territory, but in 1796 it became simply Tennessee, the fifteenth state in the Union.

North Carolina Division of Travel and Tourism

THE STATE CAPITOL BUILDING

The North Carolina State Capitol is one of the finest and best preserved examples of a major civic building in the Greek Revival style of architecture.

Prior to 1792, North Carolina legislators met in various towns throughout the state, gathering most frequently in Halifax, Hillsborough, and New Bern. Meetings were held in local plantation houses, court houses, and even churches. However, when the City of Raleigh was established as the permanent seat of the Government of North Carolina in 1792, a simple, two-story brick State House was built on Union Square. The State House was completed in 1796.

The State House was enlarged between 1820 and 1824 by state architect William Nichols who added a third floor, eastern and western wings, and a domed rotunda at the building's center. The rotunda housed a statue of President George Washington by sculptor Antonio Canova, acquired by the state in 1821. When the State House burned down on June 21, 1831, the statue was damaged beyond repair.

The General Assembly of 1832-33 ordered that a new Capitol be built as an enlarged version of the old State House. The new Capitol would be a cross-shaped building with a central, domed rotunda. The sum of $50,000 was appropriated, and a building commission appointed to initiate the plan. The Commissioners for Rebuilding the Capitol first employed William Nichols, Jr. to help them prepare plans for the building. In August of 1833, Nichols was replaced by the distinguished New York architects Ithiel Town and Alexander Jackson Davis. Town and Davis greatly improved upon the earlier design, and developed a plan which gave the Capitol its present appearance.

David Paton (1802-1882), an architect born in Edinburgh, Scotland and who had worked for the noted English architect Sir John Soane, was hired in September, 1834, to superintend the construction of the Capitol. Paton replaced Town and Davis as the Commissioners' architect in early 1835. The Capitol was completed under Paton's supervision except for the exterior stone walls which were largely in place when he arrived in Raleigh.

Paton made several modifications to the Town and Davis plans for the interior. Among the changes were the cantilevered gallery at the second floor level of the rotunda, the groined masonry vaulting of the first floor offices and corridor ceilings, and the interior arrangement of the east and west porticoes.

After clearing away the rubbish of the old State House, excavations were made and a new foundation was laid. The cornerstone was set in place on July 4, 1833. After the initial foundation was laid, work progressed slowly and the original appropriation was soon exhausted. At the next session of the Legislature, an additional appropriation of $75,000 was made to continue construction. Many skilled immigrant Scottish artisans came to Raleigh and were involved in this phase of construction.

Most of the Capitol's architectural details, including the columns, mouldings, ornamental plasterwork, and ornamental honeysuckle atop the dome, were carefully patterned after features of Greek temples: the exterior columns are Doric in order and are modeled after those of the Parthenon; the chamber of the House of Representatives follows the semi-circular plan of a Greek amphitheatre and its architectural ornamentation is in the Corinthian order of the Tower of the Winds; and the Senate Chamber is decorated in the Ionic order of the Erechtheum. The only non-classical parts of the building are two large rooms on the third floor which were finished in the Gothic style that was just beginning its popularity in American architectural circles.

The ornamental ironwork, plasterwork, chandeliers, hardware, and marble mantels of the Capitol came from Philadelphia. The desks and chairs in the House and Senate Chambers were made by Raleigh cabinetmaker, William Thompson.

The Capitol was completed in 1840 at a total cost (including furnishings) of $532,682.34, or more than three times the yearly general revenues of the State at that time.

Architect David Paton gave the following description of the new edifice:

"The State Capitol is 160 feet in length from north to south by 140 feet from east to west. The whole height is 97½ feet in the center. The apex of pediment is 64 feet in height. The stylobate is 18 feet in height. The columns of the east and west porticoes are 5 feet 2½ inches in diameter. An entablature, including blocking course, is continued around the building 12 feet high.

The columns and entablature are Grecian Doric, and copied from the Temple of Minerva, commonly called the Parthenon, which was erected in Athens about 500 years before Christ. An octagon tower surrounds the rotunda, which is ornamented with Grecian cornices, etc., and its dome is decorated at top with a similar ornament to that of the Choragic Monument of Lysicrates, commonly called the Lanthorn of Demosthenes.

The interior of the Capitol is divided into three stories: First, the lower story, consisting of ten rooms, eight of which are appropriated as offices to the Governor, Secretary, Treasurer, and Comptroller, each having two rooms of the same size—the one containing an area of 649 square feet and four closets, the other 528 square feet—two committee rooms, each containing 200 square feet and four closets: also the rotunda, corridors, vestibules, and piazzas, contain an area of 4,370 square feet. The vestibules are decorated with columns and antae, similar to those of the Ionic Temple on the Ilissus, near the Acropolis of Athens. The remainder is groined with stone and brick, springing from columns and pilasters of the Roman Doric.

The second story consists of Senatorial and Representatives' chambers, the former containing an area of 2,545 and the latter 2,849 square feet. Four apartments enter from the Senate Chamber, two of which contain each an area of 169 square feet, and the other two contain each an area of 154 square feet; also, two rooms enter from Representatives' chamber, each containing an area of 170 square feet; of two committee rooms, each containing an area of 231 square feet; of four presses and the passages, stairs, lobbies, and colonnades, containing an area of 3,204 square feet.

The lobbies and Hall of Representatives have their columns and antae of the Octagon Tower of Andronicus Cyrrhestes and the plan of the hall is of the formation of the Greek theatre and the columns and antae in the Senatorial chamber and rotunda are of the Temple of Erectheus, Minerva, Polias, and Pandrosus, in the Acropolis of Athens, near the above named Parthenon.

The third, or attic story, consists of rooms appropriated to the Supreme Court and Library, each containing an area of 693 square feet. Galleries of both houses have an area of 1,300 square feet; also two apartments entering from Senate gallery, each 169 square feet; of four presses and the lobbies' stairs, 988 square feet. These lobbies as well as rotunda, are lit with cupolas, and it is proposed to finish the court and library in the florid Gothic style."

In 1970 the State acquired a duplicate of the original marble statue of Washington by Canova which is located in the rotunda of the Capitol. In niches around the rotunda are busts of three North Carolina governors - John M. Morehead, William A. Graham, and Samuel Johnston - and United States Senator Matthew W. Ransom.

Stairways in the east and west porticoes give access to the second floor, where the Senate and House Chambers and related offices are located. Rooms in the east and west wings, originally designated as legislative committee rooms, now serve other purposes. On the third floor are the galleries of the Senate and House Chambers, and in the east and west wings are the original State Supreme Court Chamber and State Library Room. Both are decorated in the Gothic Style. The domed, top-lit vestibules of these two rooms are especially noteworthy and based on designs by Soane.

The Capitol housed all of state government until the late 1880's. Today the only official occupants of the Capitol are the Governor and the Lieutenant Governor, and the Secretary of State. The Supreme Court moved to its own building in 1888 and in 1963, the General Assembly moved into the newly constructed Legislative Building. This was the first building erected by the State exclusively for use by the General Assembly.

The Capitol Today

The Capitol Building has changed less in appearance than any major American civic building of its era. The stonework, the ornamental plaster and ironwork, the furniture of the legislative chambers, and all but one of the marble mantels that visitors see today are original, not restorations or reproductions. Yet, continuous and heavy use since 1840 has left its mark on

14

North Carolina Division of Travel and Tourism

the building, and to cope with this wear and tear, the Capitol receives periodic attention. Rehabilitation work began in 1971 with the intention of preserving and enhancing the architectural spendor and decorative beauty of the Capitol for future generations. Work done included replacing the leaky copper roof, cleaning and sealing the exterior stone, and repainting the rotunda. More recently, plasterwork damaged by roof leaks was repaired, obsolete wiring and plumbing replaced, the heating and cooling systems in the upper floors were reworked to make them less conspicious, worn carpets and draperies were replaced, and the rest of the interior was repainted.

As our Nation celebrated its Bicentennial in 1976, our State Capitol was enjoying a celebration of its own. Several years of renovation work to the old Senate and House chambers and the executive offices on the first floor were completed and the Capitol was once again ready to receive occupants. Governor James B. Hunt, Jr. and some of his staff moved back in, as did long-time resident Secretary of State Thad Eure. Mr. Eure served in the Capitol longer than anyone in its history - 60 years as of his retirement in early 1989. The executives occupying the Capitol at present are Governor James G. Martin, Lieutenant Governor James C. Gardner, as well as Secretary of State Rufus L. Edmisten, who maintains a ceremonial office on the second floor.

During late 1988 and early 1989 extensive landscape and grounds renovations were begun to enhance the beauty of the Capitol and to improve its visibility. In an effort to make the Capitol more accessible to the people of North Carolina, the building has been opened to the public on weekends with guided tours available.

The Legislative Building

In 1959,the General Assembly appropriated funds for the construction of a new legislative building. The new facility was needed to accommodate a growing Legislative Branch and to provide larger quarters for legislators and staff. The act creating the building commission was passed on June 12, 1959. The Commission was made up of seven people - two who had served in the State Senate to be appointed by the President of the Senate, two who had served in the State House of Representatives to be appointed by the Speaker of the House, and three appointed by the Governor. Lieutenant Governor Luther E. Barnhardt, President of the Senate, appointed Archie K. Davis and Robert F. Morgan. Speaker of the House Addison Hewlett appointed B.I. Satterfield and Thomas J. White. Governor Luther Hodges appointed A.E. Finley, Edwin Gill, and Oliver Rowe. White was elected to serve as Chairman of the Commission and Morgan was elected Vice-Chairman. In addition to the appointed members, Paul A. Johnston, Director of the Department of Administration, was elected to serve as Executive Secretary. When Mr. Johnston resigned, State Property Officer Frank B. Turner was selected to replace him.

Edward Durell Stone of New York and John S. Holloway and Ralph B. Reeves, Jr. of Raleigh were selected by the Commission to serve as architectural consultants.

After a thorough study by the Commission, the site selected for construction was a 5½-acre area one block north of the Capitol. This site, encompassing two blocks, is bounded by Jones, Salisbury, Lane and Wilmington Streets. A section of Halifax Street between Jones and Lane was closed and made a part of the new site. Bids on the new building were received in December, 1960, and construction began in early 1961.

The 1961 General Assembly appropriated an additional one million dollars for furnishings and equipment bringing the total appropriation to $5.5 million, or $1.24 for each citizen of North Carolina based on 1960 census figures.

The consulting architects wrote the following description of the new building:

> The State Legislative Building, though not an imitation of historic classical styles, is classical in character. Rising from a 340-foot wide podium of North Carolina granite, the building proper is 242 feet square. The walls and the columns are of Vermont marble, the latter forming a colonnade encompassing the building and reaching 24 feet from the podium to the roof of the second floor.
>
> Inset in the south podium floor, at the main entrance, is a 28-foot diameter terrazzo mosaic of the Great Seal of the State. From the first floor main entrance (on Jones Street) the carpeted 22-foot wide main stair extends directly to the third floor and the public galleries of the Senate and House, the auditorium, the display area, and the roof gardens.
>
> The four garden courts are located at the corners of the building. These courts contain tropical plants, and three have pools, fountains, and hanging planters. The main floor areas of the courts are located on the first floor, and galleries overlook the courts from the mezzanine floor. The skylights which provide natural lighting are located within the roof gardens overhead. The courts provide access to committee rooms in the first floor, the legislative chambers in the second floor, and to members' offices in both floors.
>
> The Senate and House chambers, each 5,180 square feet in area, occupy the east and west wings of the second floor. Following the traditional relationship of the two chambers in the Capitol, the two spaces are divided by the rotunda; and when the main brass doors are open, the two presiding officers face one another. Each pair of brass doors weighs 1,500 pounds.
>
> The five pyramidal roofs covering the Senate and House chambers, the auditorium, the main stair, and the rotunda are sheathed with copper, as is the Capitol. The pyramidal shape of the roofs are visible in the pointed ceilings inside. The structural ribs form a coffered ceiling; and inside the coffered patterns are concentric patterns outlined in gold. In each chamber, the distance from the floor to the peak of the ceiling is 45 feet.

Chandeliers in the chambers and the main stair are 8 feet in diameter and weigh 625 pounds each. The 12 foot diameter chandelier of the rotunda, like the others, is of brass, but its weight is 750 pounds.

Because of the interior climate, the garden courts and rotunda have tropical plants and trees. Outside, however, the shrubs and trees are of an indigenous type. Among the trees on the grounds and on the roof areas are sugar maples, dogwoods, crabapples, magnolias, crepe myrtles, and pines.

Throughout the building, the same color scheme is maintained: Walnut, accented with white, gold and red, and green foliage. In general, all wood is American walnut, metal is brass or similar material, carpets are red, and upholstery is gold or black.

The enclosed area consists of 206,000 square feet of floor area with a volume of 3,210,000 cubic feet. Heating equipment provides over 7,000,000 B.T.U.s per hour; and the cooling equipment has a capacity of 620 tons. For lighting, motors, and other electrical equipment, the building has a connected service load of over 2,000,000 watts.

In the past decade additional renovations have been completed to create more office space and improve on meeting room facilities needed for the various committees of the General Assembly. In 1982, the Legislative Office Building opened and while the first occupants were the Department of the Secretary of State on the third floor and the State Auditor on the second, the majority of the space currently is used by the legislature. Nearly half of the members of each house moved to new offices in the building as well as several of the support divisions of Legislative Services.

THE EXECUTIVE RESIDENCES OF NORTH CAROLINA

North Carolina's first legislators were traveling men. With no "fixed seat of government" after 1775, early members of the General Assembly traveled from plantation to plantation and town to town until 1792 when a capital (Raleigh) was planned and laid out in the "woods of Wake." They named the new city in honor of the Elizabethan patron of early colonization, Sir Walter Raleigh. Shortly thereafter, the legislature enacted a law requiring the governor to reside at the permanent seat of government. Samuel Ashe of New Hanover County, elected in 1794, was the first Governor to come under this law. He expressed his reaction emphatically: ". . . it was never supposed that a Man annually elected to the Chief Magistracy would commit such folly as to attempt the building of a House at the seat of Government in which he might for a time reside." The Committee of the General Assembly to which Ashe's letter was referred hastened to inform him that the law was enacted before he was elected governor and could be considered "as a condition under the incumbrance of which he accepted the appointment."

Despite its pointed pronouncement, the General Assembly took steps to provide a dwelling for chief executives, instructing the state treasurer to purchase or lease a suitable house. In 1797, a plain two-story frame building painted white and an office for the governor were provided on lot 131, the southwest corner of Fayetteville and Hargett streets. The house proved hopelessly inadequate by 1810, as evinced in a letter from Governor Benjamin Smith:

> . . . But we shall have time to retrace our steps for the House allotted by the State for the Chief Magistrate is in such order that it is agreed by all who view it, not to be fit for the family of a decent tradesman, and certainly none could be satisfied; even if safe in it, but this is questionable. The late storm has thrown off a considerable part of one of the chimneys and cracked some of the remainder. The plaster is frequently falling, and the roof is so leaky that in going from the sitting rooms to the chambers during a rain a wetting is experienced.

To remedy this situation, the General Assembly of 1813 appointed a committee to provide better facilities and plans were drawn for the erection of a more suitable dwelling. The members selected a site at the foot of Fayetteville Street facing the old State house. In 1816, an elaborate brick structure with white columned porticoes was completed and Governor William Miller became the first occupant of the "Governor's Palace."

Twenty succeeding governors resided in the "Palace", as it was cynically termed, and much of the history of the state centered there. General Lafayette was an overnight guest in 1825, and some sessions of the General Assembly were held in the building following the burning of the State House in 1831. Zebulon Baird Vance was the last governor to occupy the Palace at the close of the Civil War.

General William T. Sherman and his staff were quartered in the Palace during the spring of 1865. Although as unwelcome guests they may have injured the pride of local citizens, occupying forces caused only minor damage. Years of neglect, however, had made the Palace unattractive to governors and their families. During the Reconstruction period and until the completion of the present Mansion in 1891, successive chief executives resided in Raleigh, living in rented houses, or hotel rooms, or — during two administrations — in their own homes. From 1871 to 1891, a noted Raleigh hotel, the Yarborough House, served as the unofficial residence for several governors.

Governor Vance, the last governor to have occupied the Palace, was reelected to office in 1877. In 1879, he presented the report of a commission appointed two years earlier by the General Assembly to investigate the possibilities of providing a suitable residence for North Carolina's governors. The commission was also charged with the task of selling unused state lands in, and adjacent to, the city of Raleigh. Proceeds from the sales were earmarked for the construction of a house and outbuildings suitable for the governor.

Opinions varied concerning the proposed project. In the matter of location, several members thought it advantageous to build the Mansion on a lot adjacent to the Capitol but were convinced the commission did not have the authority to do so. Others favored building an executive mansion on Burke Square, while the majority wanted to renovate the old Palace. Despite spirited debates, the commission did agree that without a special appropriation a new house could be built through the sale of the Palace and other state property. Because of the general lack of unanimity, however, the commission merely reported its accomplishments and awaited further legislative orders.

The decision to build the present Executive Mansion was finally approved by the General Assembly through the efforts and perseverance of Governor Thomas J. Jarvis (1879-1885). A bill ratified in February 1883, authorized the construction of a house on Burke Square, provided some furnishings, and required the governor to occupy it upon its completion. The governor and the Council of State were directed to use convict labor and such materials as were "manufactured or prepared, either in whole or in part" at the penitentiary, when such a procedure seemed feasible. Governor Jarvis felt there might be some differences of interpretation of the statement. He reasoned that with the recent completion of the state penitentiary a saving could be realized through the purchase of large quantities of building materials and the employment of convict labor in the construction of the Mansion. From a practical standpoint, Jarvis thought the state would profit by having both of the projects under the same management. Experienced businessmen advised that such a plan might save the state up to $20,000.

The penitentiary board, realizing the law required it to furnish the major portion of labor and materials for the Executive Mansion, authorized the warden to make a contract for $25,000. The Council of State accepted this arrangement. Two months after passage of the bill, the Council of State met

20

North Carolina Division of Travel and Tourism

with the governor to discuss financing the project. The governor was to use money from an earlier (1877) sale of state lands, to sell the old Palace and grounds, and to employ an architect to draft sketches and specifications for the council's consideration. Expenditures were not to exceed the funds available and money spent by the governor and council was to be placed in an itemized account under the strict supervision of the auditor.

Nominees for an architect were then considered. The superintendent of construction for the State Capitol, David Paton, was suggested, but because of the architect's advanced age, he was passed over for the assignment. The council selected Samuel Sloan of Philadelphia and his assistant, Gustavus Adolphus Bauer, and received Sloan's designs from him personally when he arrived in Raleigh on April 28, 1883. These were declared "very artistic," representing "an ornate building, in modern style, three stories in height, with the ample porches, hallways and windows which every house built in this climate should have." On May 7, the Sloan designs were accepted with minor modifications suggested by some of Raleigh's "able builders."

During the early stages of construction, a report issued by the officers of the penitentiary board, in mid-1884, declared the building "handsome in design, constructed of the best material by the best workers." Employment of convict labor on state projects was not a new idea. Working on the Mansion must have seemed pleasurable compared to the back-breaking repair work on the state-owned railroad. Masons used pressed brick made at the prison for the construction of the Mansion and later for the walks surrounding it. At the end of each day, each crew leader at the brickyard signed his name or initialed his stacks of brick to indicate the number his crew had made. The exterior of the Mansion was trimmed with North Carolina sandstone. Prison officials expressed satisfaction with the artistry and convenience of the interior of the house and wished to enhance it further by using "an elaborate North Carolina hardwood finish." A second progress report issued by Governor Jarvis in 1885, stated that stone for the residence was quarried in Anson County. The governor also favored the use of native hardwoods in the ceiling, wainscoting, and woodwork of the first floor.

As soon as the Mansion was reported complete, the Council of State met. The attorney general announced that the Board of Public Buildings and Grounds would supervise upkeep of the property under the direction of the keeper of the Capitol. In November 1889, before the Mansion was occupied, repair and preservation work had already begun with "certain exterior and interior painting" of the woodwork. Most of the accounts emphasize the deplorable condition of the completed house, including cheap plumbing and dirt used as soundproofing beneath floors. The third floor and the basement had been left unfinished. On the Mansion grounds were stables for "horses driven to the governor's carriage" and other dependencies. Drinking water was pumped by a small gasoline engine from two cisterns in the basement to a tank located on the third floor.

By December 1890 the Mansion was nearly finished; but Governor Daniel Fowle (1889-1891) did not move in until early January 1891. He was par-ticularly anxious to occupy the house in view of earlier attempts to abandon it as a residence for the governor. Fowle brought his own furniture to make up the deficit in the Mansion, setting a precedent followed for many years before the house was adequately furnished. Moving from a sixteen-room house to one with more than thirty rooms made furnishing the residence a sizable problem.

The earliest laws providing for construction of a governor's residence called for the purchase of furnishings. As the costs of construction mounted, only a small portion of the funds set aside for furniture remained. Some purchases were made by Governor and Mrs. Jarvis as early as 1883, and Governor Scales reported in 1887 that he had obtained some furniture from the old Palace. Further purchases were made with an appropriation of $1,500 in 1891. To avoid confusion over ownership of the Mansion furnishings, Fowle methodically filed a list of his personal belongings with the state treasurer. Governor Fowle's term of office was cut short by his sudden death on April 7, 1891, only three months after he had moved into the Mansion. His term was filled by his successor, Lieutenant-Governor Thomas Holt.

Elias Carr was the first governor to live in the Mansion for a full four-year term (1893-1897). Like his predecessors, he found the house in need of furnishings and repairs. Funds were allocated by the legislature in February 1893 for the completion of the Mansion and interior improvements. Two years later, another appropriation made landscaping the grounds possible.

Shortly after the inauguration of Governor Daniel Russell (1897-1901), the General Assembly appointed a committee to examine the Mansion and recommend needed alterations. The committee found that minor repairs were needed and promptly introduced a resolution to provide the necessary money. In March 1897 an appropriation of $600 was allotted for the Mansion's upkeep.

At the close of the nineteenth century, a permanent residence for the state's chief executives more commodious than its predecessors had at last been established in the capital. While the Mansion reflected the progressive vitality and spirit of North Carolina and its people, it needed constant upgrading and maintenance to keep it in step with the times — an evolutionary process which continued into the next century.

With the dawn of a new century, North Carolina's governors moved the state forward with progressive new programs designed to benefit a society which remained predominantly agricultural. Of primary importance was upgrading the educational system and the establishment of industries bringing new jobs and added revenues to the state. The administrations of Governors Aycock, Glenn, Kitchin, and Craig emphasized these aims. During their terms, the Executive Mansion continued to serve as the center of Tar Heel hospitality. The need for major repairs to the residence, however, became more evident as year passed.

As frequently seemed the case with new governors, Thomas Bickett's term (1917-1921) began with an inspection of the Mansion and recommendations for improvement. The superintendent of buildings and grounds made a detailed report, and Mrs. Bickett submitted suggestions for interior renovations by architect James A. Salter, with his estimates of cost. Her plea resulted in the introduction of a bill which requested $65,000 for repairs and renovations. This optimistic bill failed to pass the General Assembly and a substitute measure was enacted in March 1917 allowing $4,000 "to renovate, equip and properly furnish the Governor's Mansion and improve the surrounding grounds." The 1919 legislature appropriated another $4,000 for continued refurbishment. During the 1920 renovation, the second floor ballroom, which had been used to house overnight groups of up to sixty soldiers during World War I, was divided by walls to form bedrooms, baths, closets, and a private corridor to connect several of the family bedrooms. Some additions to the furnishings were made. Mrs. Bickett purchased dining room furniture and a four-poster bed for the guest room at the top of the Grand Staircase — the room where President Harry S. Truman was to sleep in 1948.

As preparations were made for Governor Angus W. McLean's residence in the Mansion (1925-1929), the previous renovations were considered inadequate. Sentiment for removing the house and landscaping Burke Square as a public park was once again aroused. Secretary of State W. N. Everett halted the movement. He had made his own examination and reported that major repairs were needed to provide the governor with a comfortable dwelling. Everett suggested a sum of $50,000 for repairs and new furnishings. Although this action was taken without McLean's knowledge, upon learning of it, he soon became active in seeking the appropriation. Thus, Everett and Governor McLean must be credited not only with saving the Mansion but also with making it, for the first time, a house in keeping with the dignity of the governor and his office.

The State Board of Health, required to inspect all state institutions for sanitation, inspected the Mansion in February 1925, shortly after McLean's inauguration. The inspection report was startling. Rated on the same basis as hotels, the Mansion received "the very low rating of 71." The report added that the management of a hotel receiving such a rating would be subject to indictment. The principal deductions in scoring were for uncleanliness.

Dust pervaded the atmosphere — covering the woodwork, filming the furniture, and stifling the air. Governor Fowle's contemporaries had described clouds of dust following in the walker's footsteps. From his time until the revealing inspection, little had been done to alleviate the condition. The basement, extending beneath the entire house, had a dirt floor with the exception of two small rooms floored with decaying wood. This deficiency allowed dirt to filter up through the unclosed registers of an earlier heating system. The hot water heater room and its entrance were paved with worn, irregular bricks which, without proper drainage, weakened the foundations of the Mansion.

The first floor walls and floors were unsound and the ornate plasterwork was disintegrating in some areas. From the small, poorly equipped, and inadequately ventilated kitchen area, cooking odors and greasy smoke were released into adjoining rooms, causing frequent embarrassment to the state's first family.

The upstairs floors, with boards five and six inches in width, of uneven and poor material, had half-inch cracks between them. Plumbers and steam-fitters had removed these boards during earlier repairs, not bothering to nail them down. They would spring and creak when walked on and were practically impossible to keep clean. In the governor's room, the carpet was nearly worn through because of the uneven surface of the floor. The bathrooms with linoleum flooring, papered walls, antique plumbing, and inaccessible corners were equally impossible to clean. The third or attic floor remained unfinished. Dust from large piles of rubbish and lime mortar sifted through ceiling light fixtures and wire openings into the bedrooms and baths below.

Consultants suggested obvious remedies: a concrete floor, drains, and ceiling for the basement; painting the ceilings and walls of the kitchen and butler's pantry; enlargement of the kitchen with new floors and proper equipment, including a ventilator and smoke hood for the stove; refinishing floors or laying new floors; closing old heat registers and openings in the walls; tiling and wainscoting bathrooms and installation of modern plumbing and electrical fixtures; properly sealing lighting fixture openings in ceilings; and covering floors with an inexpensive but serviceable material.

When money became available, the architectural firm of Atwood and Nash was employed to carry out the renovations. H. Pier-Giavina, a "decorative artist" of Wilmington, N.C., aided in the interior decoration. He recommended ivory, or some other light color, for the first floor woodwork. Pier-Giavina ordered round rosettes to cover openings in the walls. In some instances, workers removed as many as seven layers of wallpaper in order to carry out the new scheme. For added safety, contractors enclosed the plumbing and electrical wiring of the kitchen within the walls.

Elizabeth Thompson, a local interior decorator, aided in the refurbishment with additional suggestions by Mrs. McLean. Workers bundled up and shipped off discarded rugs to be rewoven; old furniture to be reupholstered; and purchased new carpets and draperies out of the annual appropriation for the upkeep of the Mansion. Governor McLean also found money to finish a part of the third floor as servants' quarters. In addition, workers installed a cloak room for women on the first floor and added a gentlemen's cloak room, a servant's room, and offices for the governor in the basement.

Written expressions recognized the greatly increased value of the Mansion. In July 1926, a letter to Insurance Commissioner Stacy Wade from Governor McLean stated that the $80,000 evaluation of the house was inadequate and that the Mansion could not be replaced for less than $200,000. The house had been constructed of the finest materials and the interior, within the past year, had been completely renovated. A newspaper account, lauding Governor McLean's accomplishments, claimed that renovating a building considered eligible for demolition had saved the state more than a third of a million dollars.

The renovation undertaken by Governor McLean was not fully completed during his term of office. Governor-elect O. Max Gardner (1929-1933) asked the Board of Public Buildings and Grounds to confer with the McLeans to determine the Mansion's needs and the General Assembly established a

"Special Furniture and Equipment Account Available for [the] Incoming Governor." At the beginning of the Gardner administration, the General Assembly authorized the State Highway Commission to build and maintain walkways and drives "within the Mansion Square." Included in this project was a plan for the landscaping of the Mansion grounds. The state contracted a prominent Philadelphia landscape architect, Thomas W. Sears, for the work. At Mrs. Gardner's suggestion, the exterior woodwork of the house was painted brown to blend with the sandstone and brickwork.

Later administrations brought further improvements and added comforts in order to keep pace with the times. An elevator was installed, air conditioning units were placed in some rooms; and a bomb shelter was added during Governor Luther H. Hodges' term (1954-1961). Mrs. Terry Sanford added many antique furnishings during her husband's term of office (1961-1965). Although the state endeavored to make the Mansion functional and livable, the legislature appropriated no money for major projects. Therefore, in early 1965, Mrs. Dan K. Moore appointed an Executive Mansion Fine Arts Committee. In August, she announced that Mrs. John Pearce of Washington, D.C., the first curator of the White House, had been employed as consultant to the Fine Arts Committee. In November 1965, Mrs. Pearce conducted the committee on a detailed tour of the Mansion and made specific suggestions for each room. Following a suggestion of Mrs. Pearce, Mrs. Moore and the Executive Mansion Fine Arts Committee sponsored a tea in June 1966, to solicit funds for Mansion furnishings. Guests received brochures listing fine antique and reproduction furniture, rugs, and accessories suggested for purchase through donations. In 1967 the General Assembly officially created the Executive Mansion Fine Arts Commission (EMFAC) thus perpetuating the program of the first committee. Six years later (1973), the General Assembly returned the commission to its original committee form.

A previously neglected area of the Mansion was the central hallway at the head of the Grand Staircase. Mrs. Moore conceived the idea of furnishing the area with representative pieces in recognition of North Carolina as the "furniture capital of the world." She contacted manufacturers who, in turn, requested the American Institute of Interior Designers to plan the area. Industries contributed furniture, accessories, and services to reappoint the hallway as an attractive and comfortable living area for the governor and his family. Another area receiving special attention was the acquisition of a North Carolina collection of books for the Mansion library. Volumes by Tar Heel authors as well as books about the state and her citizens were acquired in the late 1960s.

A legislative appropriation of $58,000 financed renovation of the institutional kitchen facilities, providing a new food freezer, expansion of the food preparation area to the basement, and a dumbwaiter-conveyor belt system to move trays from the first floor. Extension of the garage area, landscaping, and lighting of the grounds contributed to the efficiency and beauty of the Mansion. For added security, a decorative brick and wrought iron wall was constructed around the perimeter of Burke Square in early 1969.

Governor Robert W. Scott (1969-1973) appreciated the historical significance of the building but felt it was time to review the Mansion's practical uses. The governor pointed out the old cast-iron radiators controlled by a single thermostat, overloaded electrical circuits, the lack of a fire escape, and other hazards which needed correction. The front entrance hall chandelier which had fallen in 1969 (fortunately without injuring anyone) aptly illustrated his concerns. Because of inadequate living conditions in the Mansion, a seven-member Executive Residence Building Commission was established by the 1971 General Assembly to develop and submit plans for a new official residence for the chief executive. The governor appointed an advisory committee including former first ladies, state agency heads, and the mayor of Raleigh to work with the commission. Members of the commission traveled to eight other states to inspect executive residences and mansions and received presentations from six architectural firms being considered for the project. Upon review of the proposed designs for a new Executive Mansion, the legislature was informed that it would be more feasible to renovate the Burke Square residence than to construct a modern dwelling.

In May 1973 the General Assembly ratified "An Act to Appropriate Funds to Renovate the Governor's Mansion and to Make It Suitable as Both a Public and Private Residence for the Governor." This act included:

— Removal of the existing heating system and installation of a year-round climate control system;
— Rewiring of the structure and its fixtures as needed to provide a safe, adequate, and convenient electrical system;
— Renovation and waterproofing of all bathroom facilities;
— Restoration of exterior brick, mortar, and wood trim;
— Construction of a stair tower on the southeast corner providing a fireproof passage from the upper floors;
— Reconstruction, repair, and weatherstripping of all window units;
— Installation of a convenience kitchen for the First Family on the second floor.

This renovation was the most extensive in the history of the Executive Mansion. The General Assemblies of 1973 and 1975 appropriated funds amounting to $845,000. Governor James E. Holshouser, Jr., and his family relinquished use of the Mansion and moved into a temporary home in the Foxcroft suburb of Raleigh for eight months while interior renovations were carried out by F. Carter Williams, a local architectural firm. Because of the size and complexity of the project, Marie Sharpe Ham, the state interior design consultant, and the staff of the Division of Archives and History assisted.

As work proceeded, it was learned that most of the deterioration had been caused by water seepage within the walls. Portions of the decorative plaster ceilings had to be reconstructed and exterior and interior woodwork repaired or replaced with materials removed from elsewhere in the Mansion. The Grand Staircase was found to be constructed of rare North Carolina heart pine. Research showed that the wood had originally been varnished and stained. An unpainted pine mantel on the third floor served as a guide for refinishing the staircase. Also, original carved paneling beneath windows and above doorways was discovered behind false panels which were removed in order to keep intact these unique design features.

In an effort to save money and promote state industry, materials produced within North Carolina were used in the renovation. Brick for the stair tower was selected to match that of the exterior. The state's textile industry assisted in replacing carpets and draperies. In addition, individuals and businesses donated decorative pieces for the enrichment of the furnishings collection (managed by the Department of Cultural Resources). Mrs. Holshouser later stated, "Our determination to emphasize North Carolina products clearly carries through the theme that Governor Jarvis had when he first envisioned a new Executive Mansion." [This determination carried over to the administration of Governor James B. Hunt, Jr. (1977-1985). A recent addition to the Mansion is a recreation room located on the third floor — a retreat for the sports-minded Hunt family.]

North Carolina has one of the few governor's residences in the nation constructed in the nineteenth century and still in use. Architecturally, the Mansion exemplifies the Queen Anne Cottage style popular during the American Victorian Period while the exterior wooden ornamentation is typical of the Eastlake style. The Executive Mansion reflects the past and stands solidly to face the future. For over 100 years, the time, talent, funds, and devotion of North Carolinians have contributed to the continuing tradition of gracious hospitality to all who enter its doors.

Governor James B. Hunt (1977-1985) was the first governor of this state who was elected to two successive four-year terms. The Mansion served as an adjunct to his Capitol office and served as a regular meeting place for his cabinet and staff. Additions to the Mansion included a chair lift for handicapped visitors, the enclosure of the back porch as a morning room and breakfast area, and the refurbishing of some first and second floor rooms as well as a recreation area on the third floor. In 1983, an executive guest residence was established at the Bailey-Tucker House on East Lane Street.

Governor James G. Martin (1985-1993) became the second chief executive to serve successive terms. As the Mansion entered its second century of service to North Carolina's governors, a Victorian garden was established south of the Mansion and was financed by private contributions. A major interior refurbishment was carried out to commemorate the building's centennial and for the viewing pleasure of over 50,000 annual visitors. The Executive Mansion stands today rooted in the past, but well appointed and equipped to meet the expanding needs and challenges of the future.

THE MECKLENBURG DECLARATION OF 20TH MAY, 1775*

OFFICERS

Abraham Alexander, Chairman
John McKnitt Alexander

DELEGATES

Col. Thomas Polk	Ezra Alexander	Waightsill Avery
Ephriam Brevard	William Graham	Benjamin Patton
Hezekiah J. Balch	John Quary	Mathew McClure
John Phifer	Abraham Alexander	Neil Morrison
James Harris	John McKnitt Alexander	Robert Irwin
William Kennon	Hezekiah Alexander	John Flenniken
John Ford	Adam Alexander	David Reese
Richard Barry	Charles Alexander	Richard Harris, Sen.
Henry Downs	Zacheus Wilson, Sen.	

The following resolutions were presented:

1. *Resolved.* That whosoever directly or indirectly abetted or in any way form or manner countenanced the unchartered and dangerous invasion of our rights as claimed by Great Britain is an enemy to this country, to America, and to the inherent and inalienable rights of man.

2. *Resolved.* That we the citizens of Mecklenburg County, do hereby dissolve the political bonds which have connected us to the mother country and hereby absolve ourselves from all allegiance to the British Crown and abjure all political connections contract or association with that nation who have wantonly trampled on our rights and liberties and inhumanly shed the blood of American patriots at Lexington.

3. *Resolved.* That we do hereby declare ourselves a free and independent people, are, and of right ought to be a sovereign and self-governing association under the control of no power other than that of our God and the General Government of the Congress to the maintenance of which independence we solemnly pledge to each other our mutual cooperation, our lives, our fortunes, and our most sacred honor.

4. *Resolved.* That as we now acknowledge the existence and control of no law or legal officer, civil or military within this County, we do hereby ordain and adopt as a rule of life all, each and every of our former laws—wherein nevertheless the Crown of Great Britain never can be considered as holding rights, privileges, immunities, or authority therein.

5. *Resolved.* That it is further decreed that all, each and every Military Officer in this County is hereby reinstated in his former command and authority, he acting comfortably to these regulations. And that every member present of this delegation shall henceforth be a civil officer, viz., a justice of the peace, in the character of a "committee man" to issue process, hear and determine all matters of controversy according to said adopted laws and to preserve peace, union and harmony in said county, and to use every exertion to spread the love of Country and fire of freedom throughout America, until a more general and organized government be established in this Province.

---

*This document is found in Vol. IX, pages 1263-65 of the *Colonial Records of North Carolina*; however, the authenticity of the declaration has become a source of controversy among historians. The controversy arises because the text of the Resolves was recalled from memory by the clerk some twenty years after the Mecklenburg meeting. The original notes had been lost in a fire.

CHAPTER TWO
North Carolina Symbols

THE GREAT SEAL OF THE STATE OF NORTH CAROLINA

A seal for important documents was used before the government was ever implemented in North Carolina. During the colonial period North Carolina used successively four different seals. Since independence six seals have been used.

Shortly after King Charles II issued the Charter of 1663 to the Lords Proprietors, a seal was adopted to use in conjunction with their newly acquired domains in America. No official description has been found of the seal but it can be seen in the British Public Record Office in London. The seal had two sides and was three and three-eighths inches in diameter. The impression was made by bonding two wax cakes together with tape before being impressed. The finished impression was about one-fourth inch thick. This seal was used on all official papers of the Lords Proprietors of Carolina, embracing both North Carolina and South Carolina.

Seal of the Lords Proprietors of Carolina

When the Government of Albemarle was organized in 1665, it adopted for a seal the reverse side of the seal of the Lords Proprietors. Between the coat-of-arms, the word A-L-BE-M-A-R-L-E was fixed in capitals, beginning with the letter "A" between the Craven arms and those of Lord John Berkeley.

The Albemarle seal was small, only one and seven-sixteenths inches in diameter and had only one face. The seal was usually impressed on red wax,

**Seal of the Government of Albemarle and Province
of North Carolina, 1665-1730**

but was occasionally seen imprinted on a wafer stuck to the instrument with
soft wax. The government for Albemarle County was the first to use the seal;
however, as the colony grew, it became the seal of the entire Province of
North Carolina. It continued in use until just after the purchase of North
Carolina by the crown. During the troublesome times of the Cary Rebellion,
the Albemarle seal was not used. Instead, Cary used his family arms as a
seal for official papers. William Glover used his private seal during his
presidency as well.

When North Carolina became a Royal Colony in 1729, the old "Albemarle"
seal was no longer applicable. On February 3, 1730, the Board of Trade
recommended that the king order a public seal for the Province of North
Carolina. Later that same month, the king approved the recommendations
and ordered that a new seal be prepared for the Governor of North Carolina.
On March 25, the Board of Trade presented the king with a draft of the
proposed seal for his consideration. The king approved the proposed new
seal on April 10 with one minor change - "Georgius Secundus" was to be
substituted for the original "Geo.II." The chief engraver of seals, Rollos, was
ordered to "engrave a silver Seal according to said draught . . . ."

Seal of the Province of North Carolina, 1730-1767

The arrival of the new seal in North Carolina was delayed, so when the council met in Edenton on March 30, 1731, the old seal of the Colony was ordered to be used till the new seal arrived. The new seal arrived in late April and the messenger fetching the seal from Cape Fear was paid ten pounds for his journey. The impression of the new seal was made by placing two cakes or layers of wax together, and then interlacing ribbon or tape with the attached seal between the wax cakes. It was customary to put a piece of paper on the outside of three cakes before they were impressed. The complete seal was four and three-eighths inches in diameter and from one-half to five-eighths inches thick and weighed about five and one-half ounces.

Seal of the Province of North Carolina, 1767-1776

At a meeting of the council held in New Bern on December 14, 1767, Governor Tryon produced a new Great Seal of the province with his Majesty's Royal Warrant bearing date at the Court of St. James the 9th day of July, 1767. The old seal was returned to his Majesty's Council office at Whitehall in England. Accompanying the warrant was a description of the new seal with instruction that the seal was to be used in sealing all patents and grants of lands and all public instruments passed in the king's name for service within the province. It was four inches in diameter, one-half to five-eighths inches thick, and weighed four and one-half ounces.

Sometimes a smaller seal than the Great Seal was used on commissions and grants, such as a small heart-shaped seal. or a seal in the shape of an ellipse. These impressions were evidently made by putting the wax far enough under the edge of the Great Seal to take the impression of the crown. The royal governors also used their private seals on commissions and grants.

Lord Granville, after the sale of the colony by the Lords Proprietors, retained his right to issue land grants. He used his private seal on the grants he issued. The last reference found to the colonial seal is in a letter from

Governor Martin to the Earl of Hillsborough in November, 1771, in which he recounts the broken condition of the seal. He states the seal had been repaired and though "awkwardly mended . . . [it was] in such manner as to answer all purposes."

Following independence Section XVII of the new constitution adopted at Halifax on December 18, 1776, provided "That there shall be a Seal of this State, which shall be kept by the Governor, and used by him as occasion may require; and shall be called the Great Seal of the State of North Carolina, and be affixed to all grants and commissions." When a new constitution was adopted in 1868, Article III, Section 16 provided for ". . . a seal of the State, which shall be kept by the Governor, and used by him, as occasion may require, and shall be called The Great Seal of the State of North Carolina.' It also provided for the secretary of state to countersign with the governor. When the people of North Carolina ratified the current constitution in 1970, Article III, Section 10 contained provisions for "The Great Seal of the State of North Carolina." However, the wording which authorized the secretary of state to countersign documents was removed.

On December 22, 1776, the Provincial Congress at Halifax appointed William Hooper, Joseph Hewes and Thomas Burke as commissioners to procure a seal for the State; however, there is no record that a report was ever made by this commission. The Congress provided for the governor to use his "private seal at arms" until the Great Seal for the state was procured. A bill calling for the procurement of a Great Seal was introduced in the lower house of the General Assembly on April 28, 1778. The bill became law on May 2. The legislation provided that William Tisdale, Esq., be appointed to cut and engrave a seal for the State. On Sunday, November 7, 1779, the senate granted Tisdale £150 to make the seal. The seal procured under this act was used until 1794. The actual size of the seal was three inches in diameter and one-fourth inch thick. It was made by putting

The Great Seal of the State of North Carolina, 1779-1794

two cakes of wax together with paper wafers on the outside and pressing them between the dies, thus forming the obverse and reverse sides of the seal.

An official description of this seal cannot be found, but many of the seals still in existence are in an almost perfect state of preservation.

In January, 1792, the General Assembly authorized a new State seal, requiring that it be prepared with only one side. Colonel Abisha Thomas, an agent of North Carolina commissioned by Governor Martin, was in Philadelphia to settle the State's Revolutionary claims against the Federal Government. Martin sent a design to Colonel Thomas for a new seal for the State; however, after suggestions by Dr. Hugh Williamson and Senator Samuel Johnston, this sketch was disregarded and a new one submitted. This new sketch, with some modification, was finally accepted by Governor Spaight, and Colonel Thomas had the seal made accordingly.

The seal press for the old seal must have been very large and unwieldy probably due to the two-sided nature and large diameter of the seal. Governor Richard Dobbs Spaight in a letter to Colonel Abisha Thomas in February, 1793, wrote: "Let the screws by which the impression is to be made be as portable as possible so as it may be adapted to our present itinerant government. The one now in use by which the Great Seal is at present made is so large and unwieldy as to be carried only in a cart or wagon and of course has become stationary at the Secretary's office which makes it very convenient." The seal was cut some time during the summer of 1793, and Colonel Thomas brought it home with him in time for the meeting of the legislature in November, 1793, at which session it was "approbated." The screw to the seal was two and one half inches in diameter and was used until around 1835.

The Great Seal of the State of North Carolina, 1794-1836

In the winter of 1834-35 the legislature enacted legislation authorizing the governor to procure a new seal. The preamble to the act stated that the old seal had been used since the first day of March, 1793. A new seal which was very similar to its predecessor was adopted in 1835 and continued in use until 1893. In 1868 the legislature authorized the governor to procure a new replacement Seal and required him to do so whenever the old one was lost or so worn or defaced that it was unfit for use.

The Great Seal of the State of North Carolina, 1836-1893

In 1883, Colonel S. MCD. Tate introduced a bill that did not provide that a new seal be procured but described in more detail what the seal should be

The Great Seal of the State of North Carolina, 1893-1971

like. In 1893, Jacob Battle introduced a bill that made no change in the seal except to add at the foot of the coat-of-arms of the state as part thereof the motto *Esse Quam Videri* and to provide that the words "May 20, 1775," be inscribed at the top of the coat-of-arms.

By the late 19th and early 20th century, the ship that appeared in the background of the early seals had disappeared. The North Carolina Mountains were the only backdrop on the seal, while formerly both the mountains and the ship had been depicted.

This brief history of the seals of our State illustrates the great variety and liberty that was taken in the design of the official State seal. The 1971 General Assembly, in an effort to "provide a standard for the Great Seal of the State of North Carolina," passed the following Act amending the General Statutes provision relative to the State Seal:

> The Governor shall procure of the State a Seal, which shall be called the great seal of the State of North Carolina, and shall be two and one-quarter inches in diameter, and its design shall be a representation of the figures of Liberty and Plenty, looking toward each other, but not more than half-fronting each other and otherwise disposed as follows: Liberty, the first figure, standing, her pole with cap on it in her left hand and a scroll with the word "Constitution" inscribed thereon in her right hand. Plenty, the second figure, sitting down, her right arm half extended toward Liberty, three heads of grain in her right hand, and in her left, the small end of her horn, the mouth of which is resting at her feet, and the contents of the horn rolling out.
>
> The background on the seal shall contain a depiction of mountains running from left to right to the middle of the seal. A

The Great Seal of the State of North Carolina, 1971-1984

side view of a three-masted ship shall be located on the ocean and to the right of Plenty. The date "May 20, 1775" shall appear within the seal and across the top of the seal and the works "esse quam videri" shall appear at the bottom around the perimeter. No other words, figures or other embellishments shall appear on the seal.

It shall be the duty of the Governor to file in the office of the Secretary of State an impression of the great seal, certified to under his hand and attested to by the Secretary of State, which impression so certified the Secretary of State shall carefully preserve among the records of this Office.

The late Jullian R. Allsbrook, who served in the North Carolina Senate for many years, felt that the adoption date of the Halifax Resolves ought to be commemorated on the State seal as it was already'on the State flag. This was to "serve as a constant reminder of the people of this state's commitment to liberty." Legislation adding the date "April 12, 1776" to the Great Seal of the State of North Carolina was ratified May 2, 1983, with an effective date of January 1, 1984. Chapter 257 of the Session Laws of North Carolina included provisions that would not invalidate any Great Seal of the State of North Carolina in use or on display. Instead replacement could occur as the need arose.

The Great Seal of the State of North Carolina, 1984-

THE STATE FLAG

The flag is an emblem of antiquity and has commanded respect and reverence from practically all nations from the earliest times. History traces it to divine origin, the early peoples of the earth attributing to it strange, mysterious, and supernatural powers. Indeed, our first recorded references to the standard and the banner, of which our present flag is but a modified form, are from sacred rather than from secular sources. We are told that it was around the banner that the prophets of old rallied their armies and under which the hosts of Israel were led to believing, as they did, that the flag carried with it divine favor and protection.

Since that time all nations and all peoples have had their flags and emblems, though the ancient superstition regarding their divine merits and supernatural powers has disappeared from among civilized peoples. The flag now, the world over, possesses the same meaning and has a uniform significance to all nations wherever found. It stands as the symbol of strength and unity, representing the national spirit and patriotism of the people over whom it floats. In both lord and subject, the ruler and the ruled, it commands respect, inspires patriotism, and instills loyalty both in peace and war. In this country we have a national flag which stands as the emblem of our strength and unity as a nation, a living representation of our national spirit and honor. In addition to our national flag, each of the states in the Union has a "state flag" which is symbolic of its own individuality and domestic ideals. The state flag also expresses some particular trait, or commemorates some historical event of the people over whom it floats. The flags of most of the states, however, consist of the coat of arms of that state upon a suitably colored field. It is said that the first state flag of North Carolina was built on this model but legislative records show that a "state flag" was not established or recognized until 1861. The constitutional convention of 1861, which passed the ordinance of secession, adopted a state flag. On May 20, 1861, the day the secession resolution was adopted, Col. John D. Whitford, a member of the convention from Craven County, introduced an ordinance, which was referred to a select committee of seven. The ordinance stated that the flag of this State shall be blue field with a white V thereon, and a star, encircling which shall be the words, *Sirgit astrum,* May 20, 1775."

Colonel Whitford was made chairman of the committee to which this ordinance was referred. The committee secured the aid and advice of William Jarl Browne, an artist of Raleigh. Browne prepared and submitted a model to this committee and this model was adopted by the convention of June 22, 1861. The Browne model was vastly different from the original design proposed by Colonel Whitford. The law as it appears in the ordinance and resolutions passed by the convention is as follows:

38

AN ORDINANCE IN RELATION TO A STATE FLAG

Be it ordained by this Convention, and it is hereby ordained by the authority of the same, That the Flag of North Carolina shall consist of a red field with a white star in the centre, and with the inscription, above the star, in a semi-circular form, of "May 20th, 1775," and below the star, in a semi-circular form, of "May 20th, 1861." That there shall be two bars of equal width, and the length of the field shall be equal to the bar, the width of the field being equal to both bars: the first bar shall be blue, and second shall be white: and the length of the flag shall be one-third more than its width. [*Ratified the 22nd day of June, 1861.*]

The North Carolina State Flag adopted in 1885

This state flag, adopted in 1861, is said to have been issued to North Carolina regiments of state troops during the summer of 1861 and borne by them throughout the war. It was the only flag, except the national and Confederate colors, used by North Carolina troops during the Civil War. This flag existed until 1885, when the Legislature adopted a new model.

The bill, which was introduced by General Johnstone Jones on February 5, 1885, passed its final reading one month later after little debate. This act reads as follows:

AN ACT TO ESTABLISH A STATE FLAG

The General Assembly of North Carolina do enact:

SEC. 1. That the flag of North Carolina shall consist of a blue union, containing in the centre thereof a white star with the letter N in gilt on the left and the letter C in gilt on the right of said star, the circle containing the same to be one-third the width of the union.

SEC. 2. That the fly of the flag shall consist of two equally proportioned bars; the upper bar to be red, the lower bar to be white; that the length of the bars horizontally shall be equal to the perpendicular length of the union, and the total length of the flag shall be one-third more than its width.

SEC. 3. That above the star in the centre of the union there shall be a gilt scroll in semi-circular form, containing in black letters this inscription "May 20th, 1775," and that below the star there shall be similar scroll containing in black letters the inscription: "April 12th, 1776."

SEC. 4. That this act shall take effect from and after its ratification. In the General Assembly read three times and ratified this 9th day of March, A.D. 1885.

It is interesting to examine the significance of the dates found on the flag. The first date, "May 20, 1775," refers to the Mecklenburg Declaration of Independence, although many speculate the authenticity of this particular document. The second date appearing on the state flag of 1861 is that of "May 20th, 1861." This date commemorated the secession of the State from the Union, but as the cause for secession was defeated, this date no longer represented anything after the Civil War. So when a new flag was adopted in 1885, this date was replaced with "April 12th, 1776." This date commemorates the Halifax Resolves, a document that places the Old North State in the very front rank, both in point of time and in spirit, among those that demanded unconditional freedom and absolute independence from any foreign power. This document stands out as one of the great landmarks in the annals of North Carolina history.

Since 1885 there has been no change in our state flag. For the most part, it has remained unknown and a stranger to the good people of our State.

However, as we became more intelligent, and therefore, more patriotic and public spirited, the emblem of the Old North State assumed a station of greater prominence among our people. One hopeful sign of this increased interest was the act passed by the Legislature of 1907, requiring the state flag to be floated from all state institutions, public buildings, and courthouses. In addition to this, many public and private schools, fraternal orders, and other organizations now float the state flag. The people of the State should become acquainted with the emblem of that government to which they owe allegiance and from which they secure protection, and to ensure that they would, the legislature enacted the following:

AN ACT TO PROMOTE GREATER LOYALTY AND RESPECT FOR THE SOVEREIGNTY OF THE STATE

The General Assembly of North Carolina do enact:

SEC. 1. That for the purpose of promoting greater loyalty and respect to the state and inasmuch as a special act of the Legislature has adopted an emblem of our government known as the North Carolina State flag, that it is meet and proper that it shall be given greater prominence.

SEC. 2. That the board of trustees or managers of the several state institutions and public buildings shall provide a North Carolina flag, of such dimensions and materials as they deem best, and the same shall be displayed from a staff upon the top of each and every such building at all times except during inclement weather, and upon the death of any state officer or any prominent citizen the flag shall be put at half-mast until the burial of such person shall have taken place.

SEC.3. That the Board of County Commissioners of the several counties in this state shall likewise authorize the procuring of a North Carolina flag, to be displayed either on a staff upon the top, or draped behind the judge's stand, in each and every term of court held, and on such other public occasions as the Commissioners may deem proper.

SEC. 4. That no state flag shall be allowed in or over any building here mentioned that does not conform to section five thousand three hundred and twenty-one of the Revisal of one thousand nine hundred and five.

SEC. 5. That this act shall be in force from and after its ratification.

In the General Assembly read three times, and ratified this 9th day of March, A.D. 1907.

Many North Carolinians have questioned the legitimacy of having the date of the Mecklenburg Declaration, May 20th, 1776, on the flag. Historians have debated its authenticity because the lack of any original documentation. The only evidence of the Declaration is a reproduction from memory many years later by one of the delegates attending the convention. Historians' main argument, other than the non-existence of the original document, is that the Mecklenburg Resolves, adopted just eleven days after the Mecklenburg Declaration, are comparatively weak in tone, almost to the point of being completely opposite. Many historians find it difficult to believe that the irreconcilable tone of the Declaration could have been the work of the same people who produced the Resolves. Efforts have been made to have the date taken off the flag and the seal, but so far these efforts have proved fruitless. Removal from the seal would be simple enough, for the date of the Halifax Resolves could easily be substituted without changing the basic intention of the date. The flag would prove to be more difficult, for there is no other date of significance which could be easily substituted.

North Carolina Wildlife Commission

THE STATE BIRD

The Cardinal was selected by popular choice as our State Bird on March 4, 1943. (*Session Laws*, 1943 c. 595; G.S. 145-2).

The Cardinal is sometimes called the Winter Redbird because it is most noticeable during the winter when it is the only "redbird" present. A year-round resident of North Carolina, the Cardinal is one of the most common birds in our gardens, meadows and woodlands. The male Cardinal is red all over, except for the area of its throat and the region around its bill which is black; it is about the size of a Catbird only with a longer tail. The head is conspicuously crested and the large stout bill is red. The female is much duller in color with the red confined mostly to the crest, wings, and tail. This difference in coloring is common among many birds. Since it is the female that sits on the nest, her coloring must blend more with her natural surroundings to protect her eggs and young from predators. There are no seasonal changes in her plumage.

The Cardinal is a fine singer, and what is unusual is that the female sings as beautifully as the male. The male generally monopolizes the art of song in the bird world.

The nest of the Cardinal is rather an untidy affair built of weed stems, grass and similar materials in low shrubs, small trees or bunches of briars, generally not over four feet above the ground. The usual number of eggs set is three in this State and four further North. Possibly the Cardinal raises an extra brood down here to make up the difference, or possibly the population is more easily maintained here by the more moderate winters compared to the colder North.

The Cardinal is by nature a seed eater, but he does not dislike small fruits and insects.

THE STATE FLOWER

The General Assembly of 1941 designated the dogwood as the State Flower. (*Public Laws*, 1941, c. 289; G.S. 145-1)

The Dogwood is one of the most prevalent trees in our State and can be found in all parts of the State from the mountains to the coast. Its blossoms, which appear in early spring and continue on into summer, are most often found in white, although shades of pink (red) are not uncommon.

North Carolina Wildlife Commission

THE STATE INSECT

The General Assembly of 1973 designated the Honey Bee as the official State Insect. (*Session Laws*, 1973, c. 55)

This industrious creature is responsible for the annual production of more than $2 million worth of honey in the state. However, the greatest value of Honey Bees is their role in the growing cycle as a major contributor to the pollination of North Carolina crops.

THE STATE TREE

The long leaf pine was officially designated as the State Tree by the General Assembly of 1963. (*Session Laws,* 1963, c.41)

The pine is the most common of the trees found in North Carolina, as well as the most important one in the history of our State. During the Colonial and early Statehood periods, the pine was a vital part of the ecomony of North Carolina. From it came many of the "naval stores" - resin, turpentine, and timber - needed by merchants and the navy for their ships. The pine has continued to supply North Carolina with many important wood products, particularly in the building industry.

THE STATE MAMMAL

The General Assembly of 1969 designated the Gray Squirrel as the official State Mammal. (*Session Laws*, 1969. c.1207; G.S. 145-5).

The gray squirrel is a common inhabitant of most areas of North Carolina from "the swamps of eastern North Carolina to the upland hardwood forests of the piedmont and western counties." He feels more at home in an "untouched wilderness" environment, although many squirrels inhabit our city parks and suburbs. During the fall and winter months the gray squirrel survives on a diet of hardwoods, with acorns providing carbohydrates and proteins. In the spring and summer, their diet consists of "new growth and fruits" supplemented by early corn, peanuts, and insects.

THE STATE SHELL

The General Assembly of 1965 designated the Scotch Bonnet (pronounced *bonay*) as the State Shell. (*Session Laws*, 1965, c. 681).

A colorful and beautifully shaped shell, the Scotch Bonnet is abundant in North Carolina coastal waters at depths between 500 and 200 feet. The best source of live specimens is from offshore commercial fishermen.

THE STATE SALT WATER FISH

The General Assembly of 1971 designated the Channel Bass (Red Drum) as the official State Salt Water Fish. (*Session Laws*, 1971, c.274; G.S. 145-6) Channel Bass usually occur in great supply along the Tar Heel coastal waters and have been found to weigh up to 75 pounds although most large ones average between 30 and 40 pounds.

THE STATE TOAST

The following toast was officially adopted as the State Toast of North Carolina by the General Assembly of 1957 (*Session Laws, 1957*, c.777).

Here's to the land of the long leaf pine,
The summer land where the sun doth shine,
Where the weak grow strong and the strong grow great,
Here's to "Down Home," the Old North State!

Here's to the land of the cotton bloom white,
Where the scuppernong perfumes the breeze at night,
Where the soft southern moss and jessamine mate,'
Neath the murmuring pines of the Old North State!

Here's to the land where the galax grows,
Where the rhododendron's rosette glows,
Where soars Mount Mitchell's summit great,
In the "Land of the Sky," in the Old North State!

Here's to the land where maidens are fair,
Where friends are true and cold hearts rare,
The near land, the dear land, whatever fate,
The blest land, the best land, the Old North State!

THE STATE PRECIOUS STONE

The General Assembly of 1973 designated the emerald as the official State Precious Stone. (*Session Laws*, 1973, c. 136).

A greater variety of minerals, more than 300, have been found in North Carolina than in any other state.

These minerals include some of the most valuable and unique gems in the world. The largest Emerald ever found in North Carolina was 1,438 carats and was found at Hiddenite, near Statesville. The "Carolina Emerald," now owned by Tiffany & Company of New York was also found at Hiddenite in 1970. When cut to 13.14 carats, the stone was valued at the time at $100,000 and became the largest and finest cut emerald on this continent.

North Carolina Wildlife Commission

THE STATE REPTILE

The General Assembly of 1979 designated the Eastern Box Turtle as the official State Reptile for North Carolina. (*Session Laws*, 1979, c. 154)

The turtle is one of nature's most useful creatures. Through its dietary habits it serves to assist in the control of harmful and pestiferous insects and as a clean-up crew, helping to preserve the purity and beauty of our waters. At a superficial glance, the turtle appears to be a mundane and uninteresting creature; however, closer examination reveals it to be most fascinating, ranging from species well-adapted to modern conditions to species which have existed virtually unchanged since prehistoric times. Derided by many, the turtle is really a culinary delight, providing the gourmet food enthusiast with numerous tasty dishes from soups to entrees.

The turtle watches undisturbed as countless generations of faster "hares" run by to quick oblivion, and is thus a model of patience for mankind, and a symbol of our State's unrelenting pursuit of great and lofty goals.

North Carolina Division of Travel and Tourism

THE STATE ROCK

The General Assembly of 1979 designated Granite as the official Rock for the State of North Carolina (*Session Laws*, 1979, c.906).

The State of North Carolina has been blessed with an abundant source of "the noble rock," granite. Just outside Mount Airy in Surry County is the largest open face granite quarry in the world measuring one mile long and 1,800 feet in width. The granite from this quarry is unblemished, gleaming and without interfering seams to mar its splendor. The high quality of this granite allows its widespread use as a building material, in both industrial and laboratory applications where supersmooth surfaces are necessary.

North Carolina granite has been used for many magnificent edifices of government throughout the United States such as the Wright Brothers Memorial at Kitty Hawk, the gold depository at Fort Know, the Arlington Memorial Bridge and numerous courthouses throughout the land. Granite is a symbol of strength and steadfastness, qualities characteristic of North Carolinians. It is fitting and just that the State recognize the contribution of granite in providing employment to its citizens and enhancing the beauty of its public buildings.

THE STATE BEVERAGE

The General Assembly of 1987 adopted milk as the official State Beverage. (*Session Laws, 1987*, c. 347)

In making milk the official state beverage, North Carolina followed many other states including our northern neighbor, Virginia, and Wisconsin, the nation's number one dairy state.

North Carolina ranks 20th among dairy producing states in the nation with nearly 1,000 dairy farmers producing 179 million gallons of milk per year. The annual income from this production amounts to around $228 million. North Carolinians consume over 143 million gallons of milk every year.

THE STATE HISTORIC BOAT

The General Assembly of 1987 adopted the shad boat the official State Historical Boat. (*Session Laws, 1987,* c. 366).

The Shad Boat was developed on Roanoke Island and is known for its unique crafting and manueverability. The name is derived from that of the fish it was used to catch - the shad.

Traditional small sailing craft were generally ill-suited to the water ways and weather conditions along the coast. The shallow draft of the Shad Boat plus its speed and easy handling made the boat ideal for the upper sounds where the water was shallow and the weather changed rapidly. The boats were built using native trees such as cypress, juniper, and white cedar, and varied in length between twenty-two and thirty-three feet. Construction was so expensive that production of the shad boat ended in the 1930's, although they were widely used into the 1950's. The boats were so well constructed that some, nearly 100 years old, are still seen around Manteo and Hatteras.

THE STATE DOG

The Plott Hound was officially adopted as our State Dog on August 12, 1989. (*Session Laws of North Carolina*, 1989 c. 773; G.S. 145-13).

The Plott Hound breed originated in the mountains of North Carolina around 1750 and is the only breed known to have originated in this State. Named for Jonathan Plott who developed the breed as a wild boar hound, the Plott hound is a legendary hunting dog known as a courageous fighter and tenacious tracker. He is also a gentle and extremely loyal companion to hunters of North Carolina. The Plott Hound is very quick of foot with superior treeing instincts and has always been a favorite of big-game hunters.

The Plott Hound has a beautiful brindle-colored coat and a spine-tingling, bugle-like call. It is also only one of four breeds known to be of American origin.

NAME OF STATE AND NICKNAMES

In 1629, King Charles I of England "erected into a province," all the land from Albemarle Sound on the north to the St. John's River on the south, which he directed should be called Carolina. The word Carolina is from the word Carolus, the Latin form of Charles.

When Carolina was divided in 1710, the southern part was called South Carolina and the northern, or older settlement, North Carolina. From this came the nickname the "Old North State." Historians have recorded that the principal products during the early history of North Carolina were "tar, pitch, and turpentine." It was during one of the fiercest battles of the War Between the States, so the story goes, that the column supporting the North Carolina troops was driven from the field. After the battle the North Carolinians, who had successfully fought it out alone, were greeted from the passing derelict regiment with the question: "Any more tar down in the Old North State, boys?" Quick as a flash came the answer: "No, not a bit, old Jeff's bought it all up." "Is that so; what is he going to do with it?" was asked. "He is going to put it on you-uns heels to make you stick better in the next fight." Creecy relates that General Lee, upon hearing of the incident, said: "God bless the Tar Heel boys," and from that they took the name. (—Adapted from *Grandfather Tales of North Carolina* by R.B. Creecy and *Histories of North Carolina Regiments*, Vol. III, by Walter Clark).

THE STATE MOTTO

The General Assembly of 1893 (chapter 145) adopted the words "Esse Quam Videri" as the State's motto and directed that these words with the date "20 May, 1775," be placed with our Coat of Arms upon the Great Seal of the State.

The words "Esse Quam Videri" mean "to be rather than to seem." Nearly every State has adopted a motto, generally in Latin. The reason for mottoes being in Latin is that the Latin language is far more condensed and terse than the English. The three words, "Esse Quam Videri," require at least six English words to express the same idea.

Curiosity has been aroused to learn the origin of our State motto. It is found in Cicero's essay on Friendship (Cicero de Amnicitia, Chapter 26).

It is somewhat unique that until the act of 1893 the sovereign State of North Carolina had no motto since its declaration of independence. It was one of the few states which did not have a motto and the only one of the original thirteen without one.

THE STATE COLORS

The General Assembly of 1945 declared Red and Blue of shades appearing in the North Carolina State Flag and the American Flag as the official State Colors. (*Session Laws*, 1945, c.878).

THE STATE SONG

The song known as "The Old North State" was adopted as the official song of the State of North Carolina by the General Assembly of 1927. (Public Laws, 1927, *c.26; G.S. 149-1).*

THE OLD NORTH STATE

(Traditional air as sung in 1926)

GOVERNORS OF NORTH CAROLINA

GOVERNORS OF "VIRGINIA"

Name	Qualified	Term
Ralph Lane	[April 9], 1585	1585-1586
John White	[April 26], 1587	1587

PROPRIETARY CHIEF EXECUTIVES*

Name	Qualified	Term
(Samuel Stephens)		[1622-1664]
William Drummond	February 23, 1665	1665-[1667]
Samuel Stephens	_____, 1667	[1667-1670]
Peter Carteret	March 10, 1670	1670-1671
Peter Carteret	_____, 1671	1671-1672
John Jenkins	[May __], 1672	1672-1675
Thomas Eastchurch	October __, 1675	1675-1676
[Speaker-Assembly]	[Spring, 1676]	1676
John Jenkins	March __, 1676	1676-1677
Thomas Eastchurch		
Thomas Miller	July __, 1677	1677
[Rebel Council]	December __, 1677	1677-1679
Seth Sothel		
John Harvey	July __, 1679	1679
John Jenkins	December __, 1679	1679-1681
Henry Wilkinson		
Seth Sothel	_____, [1682]	[1682]-1689
John Archdale	December __, 1683	1683-1686
John Gibbs	November __, 1689	1689-1690
Phillip Ludwell	May __, 1690	1690-1691
Thomas Jarvis	July __, 1690	1690-1694
Phillip Ludwell	November __, 1693	1693-1695
Thomas Harvey	July __, 1694	1694-1699
John Archdale	June __, 1695	1695
John Archdale	January __, 1697	1697
Henderson Walker	July __, 1699	1699-1703
Robert Daniel	July __, 1703	1703-1705
Thomas Cary	March 21, 1705	1705-1706
William Glover	July 13, 1706	1706-1707
Thomas Cary	August __, 1707	1707
William Glover	October 28, 1707	1707-1708
Thomas Cary	July 24, 1708	1708-1711
[William Glover]		[1709-1710]
Edward Hyde	January 22, 1711	1711-1712
Edward Hyde	May 9, 1712	1712
Thomas Pollock	September 12, 1712	1712-1714

---

*The names indented first are those who served as chief executive but were appointed either deputy or lieutenant governor. Those indented second served while president of the council.

Name	Qualified	Term
Charles Eden	May 28, 1714	1714-1722
Thomas Pollock	March 30, 1722	1722
William Reed	September 7, 1722	1722-1724
George Burrington	January 15, 1724	1724-1725
Edward Moseley	October 31, 1724	1724
Sir Richard Everard	July 17, 1725	1725-1731

ROYAL CHIEF EXECUTIVES

Name	Qualified	Term
George Burrington	February 25, 1731	1731-1734
Nathaniel Rice	April 17, 1734	1734
Gabriel Johnston	November 2, 1734	1734-1752
Nathaniel Rice	July 17, 1752	1752-1753
Matthew Rowan	February 1, 1753	1753-1754
Arthur Dobbs	November 1, 1754	1754-1765
James Hasell	October 15, 1763	1763
William Tryon	April 3, 1765	1765
William Tryon	December 20, 1765	1765-1771
James Hasell	July 1, 1771	1771
Josiah Martin	August 12, 1771	1771-1775
James Hasell	October 8, 1774	1774

ELECTED BY THE GENERAL ASSEMBLY

Name	Residence	Qualified	Term
Richard Caswell	Dobbs	December 21, 1776	1776-1777
Richard Caswell	Dobbs	April 18, 1777	1777-1778
Richard Caswell	Dobbs	April 20, 1778	1778-1779
Richard Caswell	Dobbs	May 4, 1779	1779-1780
Abner Nash	Craven	April 21, 1780	1780-1781
Thomas Burke	Orange	June 26, 1781	1781-1782
Alexander Martin	Guilford	October 5, 1781	1781-1782
Alexander Martin	Guilford	April 22, 1782	1782-1783
Alexander Martin	Guilford	April 30, 1783	1783-1784
Alexander Martin	Guilford	May 3, 1784	1784-1785
Richard Caswell	Dobbs	December 12, 1785	1785-1786
Richard Caswell	Dobbs	December 23, 1786	1786-1787
Samuel Johnston	Chowan	December 20, 1787	1787-1788
Samuel Johnston	Chowan	November 18, 1788	1788-1789
Samuel Johnston	Chowan	November 18, 1789	1789
Alexander Martin	Guilford	December 17, 1789	1789-1790
Alexander Martin	Guilford	December 9, 1790	1790-1792
Alexander Martin	Guilford	January 2, 1792	1792
Richard Dobbs Spaight	Craven	December 14, 1792	1792-1793
Richard Dobbs Spaight	Craven	December 26, 1793	1793-1795
Richard Dobbs Spaight	Craven	January 6, 1795	1795
Samuel Ashe	New Hanover	November 19, 1795	1795-1796
Samuel Ashe	New Hanover	December 19, 1796	1796-1797
Samuel Ashe	New Hanover	December 5, 1797	1797-1798
William R. Davie	Halifax	December 7, 1798	1798-1799

Name	Residence	Qualified	Term
Benjamin Williams	Moore	November 23, 1799	1799-1800
Benjamin Williams	Moore	November 29, 1800	1800-1801
Benjamin Williams	Moore	November 28, 1801	1801-1802
John Baptiste Ashe	Halifax		
James Turner	Warren	December 6, 1802	1802-1803
James Turner	Warren	December 6, 1803	1803-1804
James Turner	Warren	November 29, 1804	1804-1805
Nathaniel Alexander	Mecklenburg	December 10, 1805	1805-1806
Nathaniel Alexander	Mecklenburg	December 1, 1806	1806-1807
Benjamin Williams	Moore	December 1, 1807	1807-1808
David Stone	Bertie	December 12, 1808	1808-1809
David Stone	Bertie	December 13, 1809	1809-1810
Benjamin Smith	Brunswick	December 5, 1810	1810-1811
William Hawkins	Warren	December 9, 1811	1811-1812
William Hawkins	Warren	December 8, 1812	1812-1813
William Hawkins	Warren	December 7, 1813	1813-1814
William Miller	Warren	December 7, 1814	1814-1815
William Miller	Warren	December 7, 1815	1815-1816
William Miller	Warren	December 7, 1816	1816-1817
John Branch	Halifax	December 6, 1817	1817-1818
John Branch	Halifax	December 5, 1818	1818-1819
John Branch	Halifax	December 7, 1819	1819-1820
Jesse Franklin	Surry	December 7, 1820	1820-1821
Gabriel Holmes	Sampson	December 7, 1821	1821-1822
Gabriel Holmes	Sampson	December 7, 1822	1822-1823
Gabriel Holmes	Sampson	December 6, 1823	1823-1824
Hutchings G. Burton	Halifax	December 7, 1824	1824-1825
Hutchings G. Burton	Halifax	December 6, 1825	1825-1826
Hutchings G. Burton	Halifax	December 29, 1826	1826-1827
James Iredell, Jr.	Chowan	December 8, 1827	1827-1828
John Owen	Bladen	December 12, 1828	1828-1829
John Owen	Bladen	December 10, 1829	1829-1830
Montford Stokes	Wilkes	December 18, 1830	1830-1831
Montford Stokes	Wilkes	December 13, 1831	1831-1832
David L. Swain	Buncombe	December 6, 1832	1832-1833
David L. Swain	Buncombe	December 9, 1833	1833-1834
David L. Swain	Buncombe	December 10, 1834	1834-1835
Richard Dobbs Spaight, Jr.	Craven	December 10, 1835	1835-1836

ELECTED BY THE PEOPLE — TWO-YEAR TERM

Name	Residence	Qualified	Term
Edward B. Dudley	New Hanover	December 31, 1836	1836-1838
Edward B. Dudley	New Hanover	December 29, 1838	1838-1841
John M. Morehead	Guilford	January 1, 1841	1841-1842
John M. Morehead	Guilford	December 31, 1842	1842-1845
William A. Graham	Orange	January 1, 1845	1845-1847
William A. Graham	Orange	January 1, 1847	1847-1849
Charles Manly	Wake	January 1, 1849	1849-1851
David S. Reid	Rockingham	January 1, 1851	1851-1852
David S. Reid	Rockingham	December 22, 1852	1852-1854
Warren Winslow	Cumberland	December 6, 1854	1854-1855

Name	Residence	Qualified	Term
Thomas Bragg	Northampton	January 1, 1855	1855-1857
Thomas Bragg	Northampton	January 1, 1857	1857-1859
John W. Ellis	Rowan	January 1, 1859	1859-1861
John W. Ellis	Rowan	January 1, 1861	1861
Henry T. Clark	Edgecombe	July 7, 1861	1861-1862
Zebulon B. Vance	Buncombe	September 8, 1862	1862-1864
Zebulon B. Vance	Buncombe	December 22, 1864	1864-1865
William W. Holden	Wake	May 29, 1865	1865
Jonathan Worth	Randolph	December 15, 1865	1865-1866
Jonathan Worth	Randolph	December 22, 1866	1866-1868

ELECTED BY THE PEOPLE — FOUR-YEAR TERM

Name	Residence	Qualified	Term
William W. Holden	Wake	July 1, 1868	1868-1870
Tod R. Caldwell	Burke	December 15, 1870	1870-1873
Tod R. Caldwell	Burke	January 1, 1873	1873-1874
Curtis H. Brogden	Wayne	July 14, 1874	1874-1877
Zebulon B. Vance	Buncombe	January 1, 1877	1877-1879
Thomas J. Jarvis	Pitt	February 5, 1879	1879-1881
Thomas J. Jarvis	Pitt	January 18, 1881	1881-1885
James L. Robinson	Macon	September 1, 1883	1883
Alfred M. Scales	Rockingham	January 21, 1885	1885-1889
Daniel G. Fowle	Wake	January 17, 1889	1889-1891
Thomas M. Holt	Alamance	April 8, 1891	1891-1893
Elias Carr	Edgecombe	January 18, 1893	1893-1897
Daniel L. Russell	Brunswick	January 12, 1897	1897-1901
Charles B. Aycock	Wayne	January 15, 1901	1901-1905
Robert B. Glenn	Forsyth	January 11, 1905	1905-1909
William W. Kitchin	Person	January 12, 1909	1909-1913
Locke Craig	Buncombe	January 15, 1913	1913-1917
Thomas W. Bickett	Franklin	January 11, 1917	1917-1921
Cameron Morrison	Mecklenburg	January 12, 1921	1921-1925
Angus W. McLean	Robeson	January 14, 1925	1925-1929
Oliver Max Gardner	Cleveland	January 11, 1929	1929-1933
John C. B. Ehringhaus	Pasquotank	January 5, 1933	1933-1937
Clyde R. Hoey	Cleveland	January 7, 1937	1937-1941
John Melville Broughton	Wake	January 9, 1941	1941-1945
Robert Gregg Cherry	Gaston	January 4, 1945	1945-1949
William Kerr Scott	Alamance	January 6, 1949	1949-1953
William B. Umstead	Durham	January 8, 1953	1953-1954
Luther H. Hodges	Rockingham	November 7, 1954	1954-1957
Luther H. Hodges	Rockingham	February 7, 1957	1957-1961
Terry Sanford	Cumberland	January 5, 1961	1961-1965
Daniel K. Moore	Jackson	January 8, 1965	1965-1969
Robert W. Scott	Alamance	January 3, 1969	1969-1973
James E. Holshouser, Jr.	Watauga	January 5, 1973	1973-1977
James B. Hunt, Jr.	Wilson	January 8, 1977	1977-1981
James B. Hunt, Jr.	Wilson	January 10, 1981	1981-1985
James G. Martin	Iredell	January 5, 1985	1985-1989
James G. Martin	Iredell	January 7, 1989	1989-1993
James B. Hunt, Jr.	Wilson	January 9, 1993	1993—